THE POCKET GUIDE TO
BADMINTON
TACTICS

Roger Mills

Bell & Hyman

The Pocket Guide to Badminton Tactics
was designed and edited by
Holland & Clark Limited, London

Designer
Julian Holland

Editor
Philip Clark

Artist
Martin Smillie

Photo Credit
All photographs by Louis Ross

Cover photo by Louis Ross: Liem Swie King
(Indonesia)

Published by Bell & Hyman
Denmark House, 37/39 Queen Elizabeth Street,
London SE1 2QB

© Holland & Clark Limited, 1985
First published in 1985

British Library Cataloguing in Publication Data
Mills, Roger
    The pocket guide to badminton tactics.
    1. Badminton (Game)
    I. Title
    796.34'5   GV1007

    ISBN 0–7135–2541–X

Phototypeset in Great Britain by
Tradespools Limited, Frome, Somerset

Produced in Great Britain by
The Bath Press, Avon

Contents

List of Diagrams

Introduction

The aim of this book is to improve your badminton whatever your standard as a player. Although there are obvious limitations to your strength and speed, to how fit you can get or how much you can develop your technique, do not despair. There is always boundless potential for improvement in the area of mental and tactical skills because game situations and opponents are as varied as life itself – each match therefore holds a new challenge for you.

As a full-time professional coach for the past 15 years, I have found myself constantly answering many of the same questions, such as "In level doubles, should I go in after flick serving?" or, "In singles what are the best replies to a low serve?", or "In

mixed, what should the man do when his partner is high-served?".

If you are an enthusiast, observer or coach you may wish to increase your knowledge, but if you are a player you can develop an "edge" to your future games. This book is designed to help you develop your mental and tactical abilities so that you can enjoy the satisfaction of outwitting your opponent, even sometimes an adversary who has a more accomplished technique.

By the time you reach the end of this book you should have found the answers to the questions above and, I hope, to all your tactical problems. Your badminton game should be much improved and you will be able to springboard into higher levels.

Points to Remember When Using This Book

1. Everything is written or drawn for right-handers, unless left-handers are specified.
2. All remarks for "he" and "man" apply equally to "she" and "woman", unless specific reference is made to male or female players.
3. Diagrams will use these *identifying symbols*:

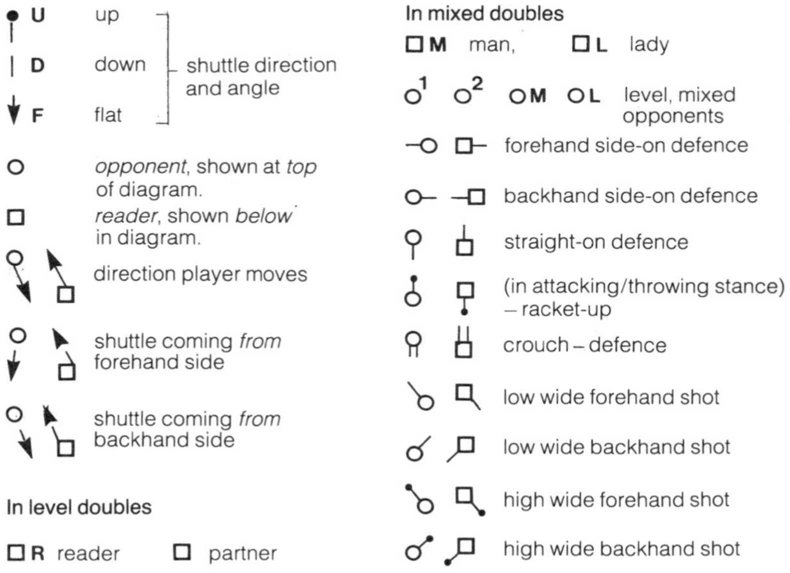

● **U**   up ⎤
│ **D**   down ⎦ shuttle direction and angle
▼ **F**   flat ⎦

○   *opponent*, shown at *top* of diagram.
□   *reader*, shown *below* in diagram.

       direction player moves

       shuttle coming *from* forehand side

       shuttle coming *from* backhand side

In level doubles

□R reader   **□** partner

In mixed doubles

□M man,   **□L** lady

○¹ ○² **OM OL**   level, mixed opponents

─○ □─   forehand side-on defence

○─ ─□   backhand side-on defence

○   □   straight-on defence

       (in attacking/throwing stance) – racket-up

○   □   crouch – defence

       low wide forehand shot

       low wide backhand shot

       high wide forehand shot

       high wide backhand shot

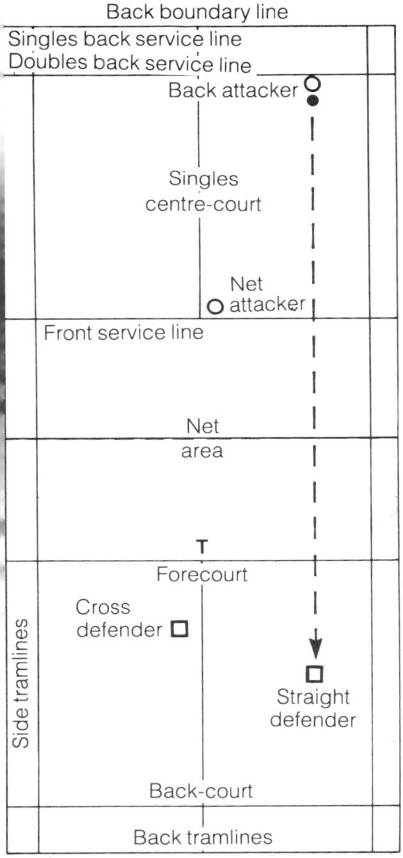

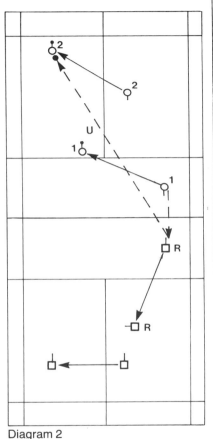

Diagram 1
Court area and positions terms

Diagram 2
Example of use of identifying symbols (Level Doubles)
Opponent O **1** plays backhand net-shot, moves across, racket-up, as net attacker Reader □ **R** forehand cross-lobs, moves back as cross-defender, backhand side-on-defence.
Partner □ straight-on defence, moves left to become straight-defender. Opponent O **2** straight-on defence, moves back, racket-up, to become back-attacker.

Definitions and Aims

Sport performance has four components – physical skills, technical skills, mental skills and tactical skills. To perform well at badminton demands a reasonably accomplished percentage of each, though this will naturally vary with the level of play required.

Whilst a complete beginner should spend time almost solely on technique with a little work on basic tactical understanding, the international will want to develop his physique and improve his mental application. For the average-experienced and club player, however, the greatest progress is likely to ensue from a concentrated effort in the areas of mental and, particularly, tactical skills.

Mental Skills

Mental skills are the abilities required to help promote a successful attitude and thus to win matches. This book will consider the importance of these abilities in so far as they affect game tactics.

Tactical Skills

Tactical skills are the abilities required to organize the moves in the game (of players and shuttle) in such a way that the chances of winning are increased.

The aim of competing is to try to win.

Your aims as a competitor should be:

1. To try to win by creating situations in which a winning stroke may be made. Gain the initiative, then the attack, then the kill (this should include forced and unforced opponent errors).

2. Learn from your defeats, otherwise they become failures.

3. Be able to win or lose graciously, always respecting your opponent.

Tactics are the most important part of the game because they give purpose to it.

Also, regardless of age, standard or event interest, singles will improve your fitness and present you with more challenges. Much of the technique and tactics that apply to singles apply equally to doubles.

If the whole court is too much for your legs to cope with, try half-court singles. You will play longer rallies, plenty of up and back movement and two singles games on one court will provide you with a tougher alternative to a club foursome.

Singles I: General Principles

TACTICS

Singles tactics are easy to learn. Look at the six principles listed below, which are easily memorized by the alphabetical initial letters:

Away from opponent.
Backhand is best.
Concentrate on errors.
Depth more than width.
Earliest shuttle always.
Fastest recovery – ready to pounce.

For the majority of players, *singles is not an attacking game*. Indeed it is fundamentally wrong to regard it as such, as will become apparent as you read on. If you want to be an attacking player you need to first "work through" fundamental play. Even if your style is already the allround attack, it is essential to be able to fall back on to the basic game against particular opponents.

AWAY FROM OPPONENT

Once you open up gaps by moving him away from centre-court, you give him problems in trying to cover the *furthest distance* from where he now has to hit (the thick arrow ➤). He will be particularly vulnerable to a quick reply back whence he came (Diags. 3 and 4) or, in his efforts to get to the *fastest reply*, to an alternative fast shot which will create movement difficulties for him (Diags. 5 and 6).

By manoeuvring your opponent away from his base and *gradually* building up the initiative, you will tire him while making few mistakes yourself. When attacking, try to hit

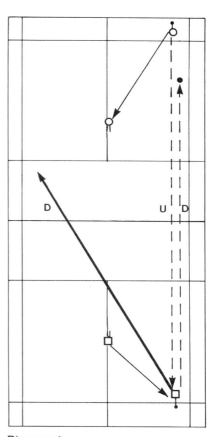

Diagram 4
Opponent put under pressure by a fast shot down to similar area from whence he came.

no more than "half-winners" away from your opponent (unless a definite opportunity to kill presents itself); you will find that in this way, you will often make winners safely.

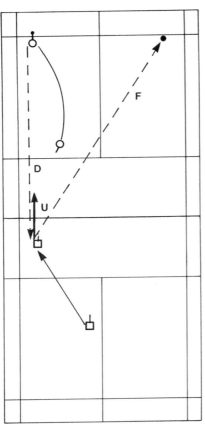

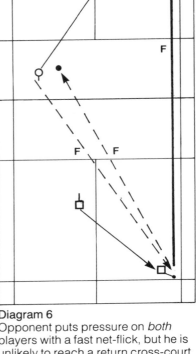

Diagram 5
Opponent put under pressure because he must move to take quickest reply, a defensive net-shot(→).

Diagram 6
Opponent puts pressure on *both* players with a fast net-flick, but he is unlikely to reach a return cross-court drop shot.

BACKHAND IS BEST

In badminton everyone's backhand is weaker than their forehand, especially if the shuttle is high and deep. It follows, therefore, that you should hit hard into your opponent's deep backhand corner as a regular (even if obvious) tactic – not too high, otherwise it will give him time to play it round-the-head.

Liem Swie King (side view) and Rudy Hartono (front view), two of the great Indonesian players, defend with a centre-court jump in the "pounce" position of readiness.

When taking up a defensive stance in the centre-court, players normally crouch in the ready position with the racket at waist height slightly towards their forehand side. Thus a smash or fast drop to a low backhand creates movement difficulties (Diag. 4), especially if hit cross-court, as your opponent is likely to have taken up an even more biased forehand defence.

Backhands are not only weaker but more *predictable*, especially when deep or wide. Diag. 8 highlights the difficulty of cross-courting from a wide smash down the backhand. Unless it can be played in front of the body, the normal reply would be a straight block (or poss-

ibly a shortish straight lob), which means you may safely approach your forehand net area (in the manner shown) to play a spinner, cross-court net-flick or knock-off.

CONCENTRATE ON ERRORS

Even in world-class singles the ratio of errors to winners is roughly 2:1, at lower levels this can increase to beyond 10:1. The majority of these errors are "unforced" and can be avoided by a closer look at the "psychology of errors".

Reducing Own Errors

1. When trying to return shuttles in desperate situations you must inevitably compromise your stroke and

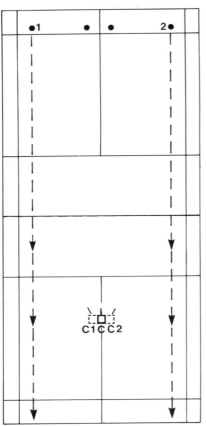

Diagram 7
Adjusting slightly singles centre-court base to cover the fastest replies.

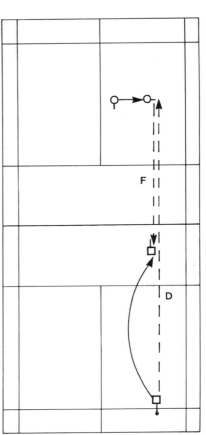

Diagram 8
Movement into net area in singles after hitting smash wide down backhand side.

get the shuttle *over the net and back into play* – a poorly executed shot going over the net is better than a well executed one into it!

2. When under pressure, you should either hit *hard and high to the middle* to give yourself time to re-

cover and narrow the angles that your opponent has to hit to the corners (Diag. 7). Or you should hit *soft and flat to just beyond the front service line* to make him play whatever early or attacking reply he can further back from the net. (Morten

Wiharjo Verawaty (Indonesia) midway during her aggressive high serve.

Prakash Padukone (India) plays a masterly round-the-head, using scissor-kick footwork with explosive grace.

Frost is the greatest exponent of this latter tactic.)

3. When serving, *take your time*. Go through a pre-serve check list (grip – racket up – look through shuttle – swing!) In order to widen the margins for error, aim very high between back tramlines into *middle of the service court*.

4. Most unforced errors occur on the second stroke of the rally, usually receiving a high serve. Try to avoid this by developing a routine which will help you to prepare yourself physically and mentally for each serve.

At the end of a lost rally, whenever possible try to reach the shuttle before your opponent and do not hit it back to him until you have got into your receiving position. This will give you time to rid yourself of any annoyance and stop him from rushing you into the next rally. As he is about to serve think *"no mistakes on this stroke"*; as you move to receive serve think *"over the net and into play"*.

Against an aggressive high serve, the least error-prone shots are the *clear* (preferably to his backhand and allowing at least a metre margin for error all round) and the straight or cross-court *half-smash* (to not closer than half a metre from the sidelines with plenty of leeway over the net). A drop shot to the net area is a particularly dangerous reply because the server is well-positioned, totally alert and is likely to read your slowish shot from between the back tramlines in time to meet the shuttle at tape height. Your drop shot would, therefore, have to be well in front of front service line *and* be deceptively executed. This combination is likely to give a very high error rate (this will apply even more if you are playing with a synthetic shuttle because, even if you are using one with a cork base, a deceptive drop shot is more difficult to play consistently).

5. Many apparently unforced errors are caused by being overconcerned about your opponent's likely reply. A lot of these can be eliminated by constructive opponent analysis (see page 26). The remainder can be reduced by continuing to allow wide margins for error and an insistence, regardless of your opposition's standard, on trying to *play your own game*.

Causing Opponent Errors

1. Look confident and determined to get the shuttle back into play whatever your predicament – he may become frustrated at his inability to hit winners or force short rallies and this could tempt him to take undue risks.

2. Concentrate on just "blunting" his attack, watching his hitting action carefully and not thinking too much about the results of your own shots except that they should continually restrict your opponent's options. Present him with "lifeless" shuttles

Nick Yates (England) plays a well-balanced forehand block.

(no angle, no pace to work on), deep and high (down the middle when in doubt) or flat ones that "die" just beyond the front service line.

3. When using any type of high serve, try to direct it more to middle of court (Diag. 7) so as to make his shot to your sidelines travel a longer distance. Resist varying the height and length and he may get bored, run out of ideas (or have too many and be undecided!) or try something different or new which will be obviously more prone to error.

Morten Frost (Denmark) plays a power forehand drive-clear from behind him, using a step-lunge.

4. If he does hit winners and/or lucky shots, quietly accept them but look confident and resolute as you continue with the same patient, war of attrition.

Ask any talented singles player the type of opponent he dislikes most and he will not talk about one with a blistering smash but one *who gets everything back*. This is because few players relish the hard physical and mental battle created by this style of opponent.

DEPTH MORE THAN WIDTH

The singles court is 30 per cent longer than it is wide; correct tactics will then be to take advantage of the court shape by using those strokes which *expose the front and back areas*. These are high serve, clear, drop shot, lob, net shot and block. You should try to improve these strokes first in your practices.

Many players do not appreciate what I refer to as "the court above", which demands an understanding of the value of hitting into a court *over the top* of the opponent.

EARLIEST SHUTTLE ALWAYS

If you always make the effort to reach the shuttle at the earliest possible moment it ensures that the opponent is put under pressure, because you allow him less time and it channels your concentration on his movement and actions so that you can read his cues much better. A real bonus is the extra time it gives you to introduce various elements of deception because your opponent *must* make *his* movement earlier.

Luis Pongoh (Indonesia) prepares for a backhand block under pressure.

Examples

With a jump lunge net-shot taken at the tape a tumbler, spinner, straight or cross-court net-flick or a cross-net shot could all be outright winners. It is almost impossible for an opponent to guard against all these potential winners (see page 24 (top)).

Jumping to intercept in the mid-court (in reply to flat clears or net-flicks) can panic opponent to get into position too quickly to defend against the threat of a mid-air smash:

Liem Swie King demonstrates a power forehand drive-clear, using a jump-lunge.

Prakash Padukone takes the shuttle early at the net with a backhand forward jump-lunge.

Liem Swie King leaps to intercept in mid-court with a jump-smash.

this leaves the way open for success with a checked-smash, punched clear or fast cross-court half-smash.

FASTEST RECOVERY

Recovering quickly to be ready for your opponent's reply is as important as the production of your stroke. So often players appear to be just standing and watching after they hit the shuttle.

This can be due to lack of techni-

Liem Swie King of Indonesia makes a smash recovery from his deep round-the-head corner look like part of a triple jump.

England's Martin Dew watches as Mike Tredgett attempts to scrape a smash off his 'inside' hip.

King waits to pounce in the forward-attacking stance as Hartono deceptively "holds" his net-shot.

King waits to pounce in the backward-attacking stance as Chen Chang Lie (China) net-flicks with considerable deception.

cal strength required to perform the recovery movement efficiently. You should develop a hitting technique which allows you to look at what is now happening on the other side of the net *as you move* into your new waiting base. This base will be either the pounce position of readiness (in centre-court about five feet behind front service line) if you have

lifted shuttle high – preparing you to push off fast in all directions but especially sideways (see page 17) – or when shuttle is returned low, preparing you to pounce forwards into net or backwards into rear court.

A legs-apart "pounce" waiting stance aids anticipation and denotes an alert and expert singles player.

Singles II: Opponent Analysis

The most important feature in planning match strategy is to decide how particular opponent's strengths and weaknesses are going to affect the way *you* play. Whilst the *safest* (and most comfortable) tactics are to *play your own game*, certain aspects of your game may suit your opponent's strengths and, unless he is playing off-form, he will turn these to his advantage.

To be able to create such a satisfying situation, you have to know your opponent in relation to your own game and current playing standard. List his strengths, weaknesses and habits in order to decide how much, if at all, you need to adjust your style of play.

It is exceptionally satisfying to know that you have done well in an important match because you planned it well.

Respect for your opponent generally is a vital philosophy. He should not be regarded as a potential frustration of your ambitions (remember, the aim of competition is to *try* to win) but as a human being co-operating with you by having similar ambitions and thereby affording you the challenge of competing.

Whatever your strategy and whatever happens in play, this respect may improve your court attitude and help you avoid too much self-criticism because you will realize that losing rallies may well be due to your opponent's skill (or even luck) rather than to your poor play.

PLANNING A MATCH
1. Have a *general* strategy as to how you want rallies to progress ensuring that your personal effectiveness is sufficiently competent for the plan.
2. Have several – but not too many – specific situations that you plan to set up.

Example
Opponent: tall, strong with attacking singles style. *Strengths:* consistent clear, heavy smash, long reach. *Weaknesses:* defensive net shots, slow reactions in defence, poor backward movement, especially recovering from net area. *Habits:* high backhand, predictably straight clears, nearly always net-flicks or lobs from net area.

Strategy
1. *General:* get him into the net area as often as possible.
2. *Specific:* low serve and attack lifted replies; straight half-smash to encourage blocks; defensive net-shots in preference to net-flicks or lobs; when in doubt, get shuttle high into his deep backhand, and go back to await straight clear.

CHANGING A MATCH PLAN
A skilled tactician should be able to alter some of his gambits and, if totally unsuccessful, his whole strategy at an appropriate moment *during the match*. It is common sense to have an alternative plan. Let us take the example above and assume that the following had happened:
1. *General:* opponent was constantly attacking the net, winning rallies with knock-offs and smashes from his left-hand court.
2. *Specifically:* by taking up a receiving position much closer to front service line, he attacked low **serve**;

his reach enabled him to lift your straight half-smashes back deep; he anticipated your net-shots and came forward early; he moved across to take round-the-head your lobs and clears into his high backhand, hitting a variety of deceptive clears and smashes.

By the time you are halfway through the first game you will know whether your opponent can cover his own weaknesses and can deal with your consequent tactics. You will also see if he has done *his* homework and has chosen a very attacking strategy.

This is the time to produce your alternative plan which may give you a chance to improve your position.

Alternative Plan

1. Well directed long, flick serves.
2. Straight smash deep, or cross-court half-smash to encourage a blocked reply.
3. Net flicks and punched clears mainly to backhand, exposing poor backward movement. If he intercepts them, the most likely reply is a drop shot.
4. Play plenty of drop shots yourself.

GENERAL TACTICAL PROBLEMS
Using Serve Variations

Generally, the aggressive high serve should be used, with the occasional low serve thrown in for surprise. This will be particularly useful if your opponent's receiving position is further back than mid-court or he drifts back during your service action.

Low serving naturally speeds the game up. This is a useful tactic against a slow, steady opponent and tends to create shorter rallies. It should be used to break up play and destroy your opponent's rhythm or can be used whenever you do not want long rallies for whatever reason.

A quickly delivered low serve, wide, especially to a weak backhand, can be an effective ploy, sometimes giving an ace, but you should usually aim for the **T** as low serves to the **T** make replies to any of the four corners travel the furthest distance. However, you would be ill-advised to do this against a player who is accomplished at "spinners" because spinning net-shots are most effective when stroked towards the *middle of the net*, and low serving to the middle make it easy for him to counter by similarly restricting *your* angles of reply.

After you have delivered a low serve, as with any other defensive stroke to the net area, you should adopt a *forward* attacking stance, this time on your centre-court base.

If your opponent displays an artful variety of responses to your low serve *and* considerable guile in his overhead replies to your aggressive high serve, a lower trajectory flicked-serve will cut down his deception. Another useful time to "throw in a quick flick" is just after an exhausting rally when you are both gasping for breath. If you hit this type of "directed" high serve to his extreme round-the-head area, he is likely to make a tired error, at that moment, with a fully extended diaphragm. You should use this sort of high serve in preference to the aggressive one whenever you want to aim to a particular area of the service court.

Drive serves at singles are indeed a rarity because the element of surprise is usually eliminated by server and receiver standing further back than at doubles. A crafty one hit quickly from a slightly wider position in the right-hand court to your opponent's backhand can be a match winner.

REPLYING TO A LOW SERVE

This poses problems to many aspiring singles players, normally because they have neither spent time practising the required strokes nor used them with any purposeful tactical application. When it becomes obvious that the opponent is going to use a low-serve game strategy, there is often a hint of panic.

The main reasons for using this strategy are to force an early error and quickly gain the attack, thereby obtaining short rallies. The main counter-strategy should therefore be to make replies that prove *difficult to attack but are relatively error free* so that normal or long rallies ensue. Even the game's top professionals (and the spectator value of the subsequent rallies) may benefit from this consideration.

This means that unless the low serve is very loose, you should not try to attack the shuttle but play it *away* from the server as follows:

1. A net-flick, that cannot be intercepted, to the *straight* corner.

2. Similarly, to the *backhand* corner (even if not straight).

3. A hairpin net-shot, *straight*.
4. Similarly, *cross-net*.

ANTICIPATION/DECEPTION

Once you are proficient at hitting and moving skills you are ready to think about *how* and *when* to move early, making reasonable guesses about likely replies.

It will help if you know something about a specific opponent's behaviour from your opponent analysis but real anticipation is about the ability to read the cues of the "display" in front of you.

You can learn to anticipate your opponent's shots by reading the signals provided:

1. Understanding the position of the shuttle within the court space and relative to opponent's starting and finishing points.

2. Observing and evaluating his whole racket-approach to the shuttle. A deceptive player is commonly associated with a "double-motion" racket action, but real deception is about the ability to reduce the cues of the "display" to your opponent.

In order not to signal *your* stroke-intention you need to:

1. Develop a wide range of strokes that can be played confidently even under pressure.

2. Develop a hitting-moving style which allows you to play different replies from similar strokes with the *same approach action*.

These are matters of technique. Tactically risk *early anticipation* against slow or accurate opponents and *more deception* against faster moving or erratic ones.

Singles III: Situation Analysis

This section highlights some of the situations you will need to analyse.

There is a mnemonic, SCALPS, which you may find useful in remembering the different points:

> **S**core.
> **C**onditions of court and hall.
> **A**wareness of other aspects.
> **L**aws of badminton.
> **P**ositions of players.
> **S**huttles.

SCORE

The position in the match should often dictate the type of play, ie when to take a breather, when to apply pressure, when to take risks, when to be steady.

Early on in the match concentrate on "finding your length" when hitting deep high serves and clears, even to the extent of hitting one just out to be sure "where the back line is".

Try out angled shots, like cross-court half-smashes and drop shots, at a time when you could, if necessary, afford to lose a few rallies "going for your shots".

Important Points

Treat going from 12–13 (or 8–9, ladies) as particularly vital because you then feel more comfortable in the knowledge that you can always choose to set if opponent catches up. Take risks going from 13–14 (or 9–10, ladies).

On game or match point *to you*, play as if it were any other important point but concentrate on keeping the shuttle in play – realize that

opponent has got to win the rally and therefore is likely to play very steadily as he cannot afford an error.

The first game or match point is always the easiest, so make sure you try particularly hard first-time-round!

On game or match point *against you*, be determined to make opponent work to win; if you do lose you will at least have left him with the memory of how hard it all was.

Then there are psychologically important points: changing up at eight in the third game and then going flat out to get at least the first rally after the change; not relaxing after winning the first game, ensuring that you get off to a good start in the second; making it quite evident, by obviously relishing some extra long rallies in the early part of the third game, that you are fit and contented to "fight to the death".

CONDITIONS OF COURT AND HALL

1. Slippery floors require a more controlled movement, whilst taking the chance of using more deception is definitely worthwhile.
2. Low ceilings will give a flatter, faster tempo of play and will make it very difficult to reply adequately to tight net play.
3. Light-coloured backgrounds will favour a more attacking policy, with a concentration on low serving and fast-hit deceptive smashes.
4. Poor or dazzling lights should be taken advantage of by specially-directed shots; the changing night and day light should receive strong consideration, particularly when you are choosing ends.

5. Temperature affects the speed of shuttles and may also determine if you should go flat out "to win in two" in extreme heat or, if cold, to get on top of a slow-starting opponent.

6. Much competitive play takes place in large multi-sports centres where heating and ventilation requirements often cause considerable disturbance to the shuttle flight. Choosing ends (starting into or against the breeze!) and adjusting stroke strength, type and direction from each end needs to be given serious thought.

7. Obstacles over the court should be noted and the relevant bye-laws for these ascertained *before* competition starts. Other obstacles, like white basketball boards attached to the walls behind court, will increase shuttle-sighting difficulty, so shots like high serves should be directed towards a different spot.

8. Generally, where the court has a favoured end, it is preferable to choose to start at the bad end. Thus you will finish at the good end after changing halfway in the event of a third game. If you are not sure if the choice of ends is important enough to relinquish choosing serve on winning the toss, then try to knock-up from the bad end and choose serve – in this way you may get both!

AWARENESS OF OTHER ASPECTS
Sports performance is affected by countless physical and psychological variables. It is important for you to understand the individual effect on *you* of even the most subtle differences in the circumstances to which you are accustomed that can cause tension and discomfort. The following are just examples to help you formulate your own list:

1. Starting time – potential arrival problems with travel, preparation, warm-up, time to get off work or school, difficulties with early morning play, business lunch before an evening match, finishing play late at night.

2. Playing times and duration – problems with deciding on which events to enter in a tournament. A day's programme needs to be carefully planned – best periods in which to have food, rest, fresh air, between-match showers. Sufficient clothing and equipment, plenty of spares (especially rackets and including sportshoes), sports first-aid kit and personal drinks-bottle.

3. Officials on and off court can have quite an influence – they are only human after all! A polite co-operative manner in your dealings with them (even though these "tactics" may appear too obvious to you!) may mean more consideration from them, when it comes to their making on or off court decisions.

4. Spectators often create an excellent atmosphere but may have a disquieting effect on your play (especially if they are more interested vocally in a game on another court!). You should never allow anyone off-court to influence adversely your technical or tactical play, or your setting or line decisions. Consideration needs to be given to seating and/or entry/passage arrangements with regard to the choosing of ends.

5. Be fully au fait with toilet facilities,

drinking arrangements and have all your spares immediately available in a bag beside the court.

LAWS OF BADMINTON

1. The method of scoring, and the fundamental sports tactics principle of "playing the percentages" should encourage you to *take risks on your own serve, whilst playing safer on opponent's serve*. In the same way as you should be saying to yourself "no mistakes" on the *second* stroke of rally when awaiting serve, you should be constantly thinking "steady" as you play your shot in a rally in which your opponent has served.

2. Setting decisions at 13 or 14 (9 or 10, ladies) may balance on many factors (eg in the second game, who has won the first; who appears to be fitter; if the player "catching up" has had a "long run" etc).

Generally, however, you should set if you are confident that you are the better player on the day, and therefore more likely to score the chosen larger number of points.

Mathematically speaking, in singles you will have the following expectation of success, assuming a 50% success rate for both players when serving:

ie assuming a 50% success rate each when serving, you should always choose to set.

POSITIONS OF PLAYERS

The area on court from which a stroke is played largely dictates the range of sensible shots available. As was emphasized on page 15, however, the opponent's position should ideally determine the final stroke choice. In general, *safe winners* should be hit:

1. In reply to short lobs/clears, a heavy smash *down the middle* (preferably "wrong-siding" his defence);

2. In reply to "killable" drop shots and blocks, a *straight* knock-off so that it does not go across the middle, where opponent is awaiting some opportunity to retrieve the shuttle back over your head.

3. In reply to "killable" net-shots, a knock-off anywhere *in* court!

The importance of net play in relation to other areas of court, from where it is far more difficult to hit winners, cannot be overemphasized. Even a beginner can hit a winner against a world champion from the net. Thus against a *much better* player you should endeavour to engage him in comparatively more net rallies.

SCORE	YOU ELECT TO	YOUR % WINNING	YOUR·% LOSING
13–13	PLAY TO 15	40	60
	SET TO 5	47	53
14–14	PLAY TO 15	33	67
	SET TO 3	44	56

SHUTTLES

The different types and makes of shuttle can change the feel of hitting, and some of the flight characteristics almost to the same extent as playing tennis on different surfaces.

Even the most sophisticated synthetic shuttles are still vastly dissimilar to feathers. Much also depends on the quality of the feathers, the width of their spread, the hardness of the cork and the type of base-covering.

Give yourself sufficient practice to become used to these differences, ensuring sole concentration for at least a week beforehand on the type and make of shuttle with which you are due to compete. A more attacking or defensive style, as well as specific shots or tactics, may be advantageous to you.

Just as an old shuttle may affect play, so too may a new one (firmer spread, crisper feel, harder cork, shinier base) – be mindful of these nuances which could cause unforced errors.

Test each new shuttle for speed, (understand Law 4), as well as flight characteristics. Hit it a few times to take the "newness" out of it.

Lapses of concentration often occur following shuttle changes (or verbal exchanges about shuttle changes!) so keep your eye on the shuttle throughout!

Summary of Singles Tactics

By way of a summary of singles tactics the basic principles are quite simple. *Singles is a game of patience and manoeuvring.* Steadiness and accuracy in shot place-

Liem Swie King prepares classically for an overhead forehand.

ment lay the groundwork for the use of speed and power.

A determination to reduce unforced errors, whether caused by poor concentration, over-ambitious tactics or inefficient technique will provide the answer to most of the questions about your present defeats in singles.

Level Doubles I: Serve and Receive

Doubles is an attacking game but the extent to which you can afford to commit yourself to a "winning" attack will depend on your relative playing standard, your individual strengths and weaknesses, and to a large extent, your sex!

The aim of doubles is to mount a successful attack as soon as possible, but what constitutes a successful attack – unless it is a winner! – depends upon what is also safe in terms of the difficulties caused by possible replies turning your opponents' defence into attack and also the potential error rate of a particular type of attack. These points become more important when you consider the fact that *scoring occurs on serve only*.

As an example let us look at the different receiving tactics in Diagrams 9 and 10. If your age, height or speed prevent you from getting back quickly enough for a flicked serve, you must obviously stand back further (at least a metre or so) behind the front service line. Having done so, if you then try to attack the low serve, in a similar way to someone who stands further up, you will increase your chances of error either into net or out at the back – and present your opponents with easier opportunities to counterattack. For these reasons *ladies doubles (at most levels) should be regarded as a game of counter-attack.*

SERVING

The first two strokes of the rally are crucial but they are not given sufficient practice time by most players.

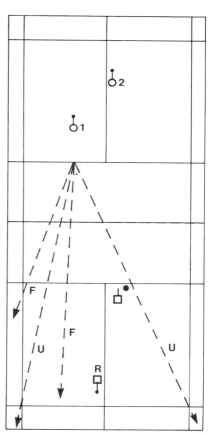

Diagram 9

□ low serves, moves in to cover net; □R stands behind mid-court as O1 is too far back to attack serve downwards, so he attacks *away* from opponents staying in forecourt to intercept replies; O2 stands ready to move back to attack, or across to defend in left-hand court.

The serving Laws give an interesting facet to the *attacking* doubles

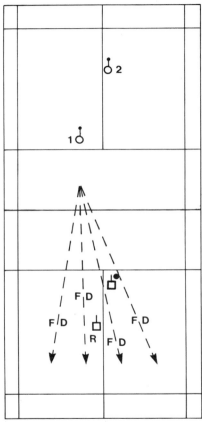

Diagram 10

☐ low serves, moves in to cover net; ☐R stands in mid-court to cover attacking replies to half-court, and intercept flicks; O1 receives near to front service line, so as to try to rush serve down middle, staying in net area to intercept replies; O2 stands ready to attack in mid-court or to move back to cover back-court.

game in that you have to start every rally from which you can win a point with a *defensive* stroke. It is impor tant to deliver serve confidently This *confidence* should be born of a knowledge of a competent, consis tent technique (obtained by regular practice), and of the *large* service court in which you can aim a verit able host of varied serves – to oppo nents whose favoured serve-returns you will already have carefully ana lysed!

The serve, however, should only be regarded as an attempt to neut ralize the advantage of the "static attack" which the receiving side automatically has as the rally is about to start.

Unless the receiver is someone who can toe the front service line you should concentrate almost solely on a low service that is drop ping from about three inches past the tape so that it falls only a few inches beyond the front service line

Where most club players low serving tactics fall short is that they stroke their serves too close to the tape, causing a disproportionate number of errors *into the net*, and too strongly so that the shuttle though crossing the net very close is "rushable" because it is *still rising* even at the front service line.

Another mistake commonly made is to plump for the safety of an accurate low serve to one spot However tight and consistent tha favourite serve is, it will always be

Nora Perry (England) shows a perfect forehand low serve (footwork and stroke).

All-England Men's Doubles Final 1983 (Malaysia *v* Scotland). Rajiv Sidek backhand serves whilst Misbun Sidek defends (above); Dan Travers receives serve whilst Billy Gilliland waits behind in attacking stance (below).

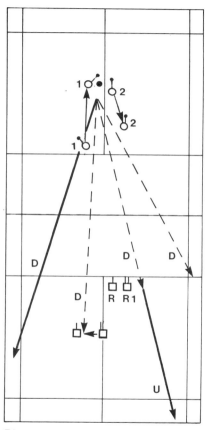

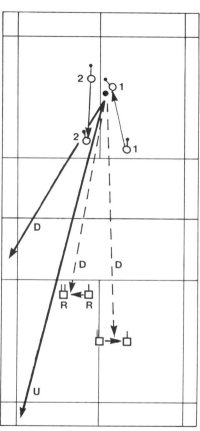

Diagram 11

Ḁ**R** drive serves down *middle* and crouch-defends against reply down same pathway; Ḁ straight-on, moves to defend *his* court; O**1** jumps back to play intercept-smash; O**2** moves towards *left* of **T** to attack net area, "concentrating" on server Ḁ**R**.

Diagram 11a

Ḁ**R** drive serves *down middle* and crouch-defends against reply down same pathway; Ḁ straight-on, moves to defend *his* court; O**1** jumps back to play intercept-smash; O**2** moves towards *right* of **T** to attack net area, "concentrating" on server Ḁ**R**.

attackable by some receivers who like it. In any case, a poor service the receiver does not expect is usually more effective than an accurate one that he does.

There is a general misconception that low serving to the **T** should *always* be favoured (because any shot to the middle line restricts the angles of possible replies) but when serving in the right-hand court, particularly to a man who toes the line, this serve, unless perfect, allows him to rush down the middle with ease (Diag. 10).

China *v* Indonesia in 1983 Thomas Cup Final. Serve and receive formations (below) with Sun Zian (serving) and Yao Ximing versus Hadinata Christian (receiving) and Liem Swie King.

Serving Positions and Stances

Apart from a variety of places to low serve towards, a variation of serving positions and stances may cause all sorts of receiving headaches. For instance, standing nearer the front line means that the shuttle flies a shorter distance giving the receiver less time to react. Also the server is aggressively nearer the net.

A service from further back has a flatter trajectory and may be more difficult for a receiver who is a "rusher" (but it is a very defensive tactic especially against a receiver who likes to play net-shot replies).

Serving from wide of the middle line creates angles and a shuttle flying even to the same spot along the front line can be awkward to deal with (Diags. 13 and 13a) interesting *low* serves can also be delivered from the tramlines.

Ray Stevens (England) forehand low serves whilst Mike Tredgett (England) prepares for its attack with a backhand defence.

Backhand versus Forehand Serving
Whilst all players may have a pre-
ferred service, it is worthwhile developing both backhand and forehand serves, not just as a variation,
but as a specific ploy against certain
opponents. Generally speaking,
Asian players favour backhand, and
European players forehand serving.

There are many technical advantages to backhand serving, but the
main tactical ones are that you can
serve from closer to the net and,
therefore, more aggressively. The
speed and variety of pace of a serve
delivered straight out of the hand is
an asset and the receiving angle can
be as different as that from a left
hander.

Variety of Serving
Traditionally, players try to obtain a
consistent tight low serve, then if,
despite practice, their technique
breaks down in competition, they
change to some sort of flat-trajectory
high serve – and hope!

If ever you have tried to receive
against an opponent who has a deceptive variety of serves, you will
understand the tactical significance
of a serving action that leaves you
totally undecided for that vital split-
second. The ability to produce a
large range of serves is all about
technique, but tactically you should
appreciate that the surprise element
causes error, uncertainty and a
possible relinquishing of the "static
attack".

An unexpected *drive serve down
the middle*, especially in the right-
hand court, will invariably result in a
downward reply in the same shuttle

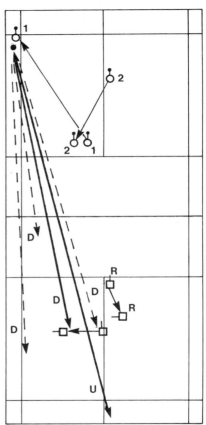

Diagram 12
□ R flick-serves *wide*, moves back as
cross-defender, awaiting drop
shot; –□ moves across to
defend; O 1 moves back for overhead
shot; O 2 moves in to *right* of T to
attack net, "concentrating" on
straight-defender –□

pathway (Diags. 11 and 11a). *Drive
serving wide* is recommended only
towards the receiver's backhand (ie

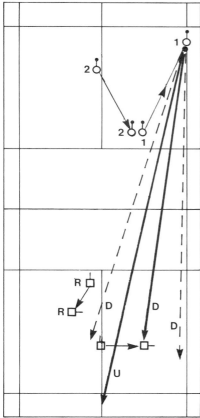

Diagram 12a

□ **R** flick-serves *wide*, moves back as cross-defender, awaiting drop shot; □– moves across to defend; **O 1** moves back for overhead shot; **O 2** moves in to *left* of **T** to attack net, "concentrating" on straight-defender □–

in left-hand court) when the likely reply will now be downward *straight*.

Whilst the threat of a *flick* serve can alter a receiver's tactics, a policy of consistent (and persistent) *flicked* serving can be used to great advantage both against speedy receivers-of-low serve, and if you *and* your partner have fast defences that can counter the subsequent jump-smash. It is also useful if you are just having a bad day with your low serve.

Successful serving tactics must not only be altered for individual opponents or specific situations but also to match the general standard of play involved. For example, beginners should serve high for most of the time because their opponents will have more difficulty attacking from further back. You can regard the *well-directed flicked serve wide* as being the best *basic serve* at all but the top level of ladies' doubles, with the low serve as variation. The flick serve puts the receiver under some movement pressure taking her out to the sides. It also stops her from attacking the server's partner's backhand, because both players will now be defending a half court each *ready to counter-attack* (possibly using crouch-defence).

Both drive and the flicked serves, despite losing the surprise element, can be delivered most effectively from the tramlines, with a pre-arranged counter-attack (Diags. 13 and 13a).

Finally, aggressive high serves (where club-ceiling heights allow) should not be ignored when, for instance, you need to take a "breather", you want to push one particular opponent to the back

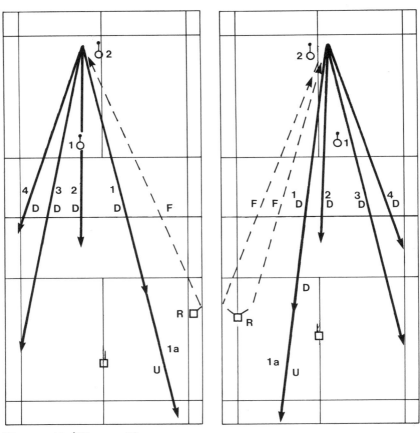

Diagram 13 / Diagram 13a

□ stands centre-court, straight-on defence prepared for smash either side, slightly biased to server's court. Receiving shuttle at such an awkward angle, even if he manages to intercept it early, ○1 will probably prefer to smash (Stroke 1) or clear (Stroke 1a) down similar shuttle-pathway; he is unlikely to opt for a drop shot down similar pathway in case server commits himself to attack net area. ○2 racket up, should initially "assume the attack", moving to T, "concentrating" on □R. If □R follows in aggressively,

□ should remain centre-court, if □R moves sideways defensively,
□ should move across to defend his own court.

court or you are the slower pair competing against a faster pair who are not heavy-smashers. This high serve has the effect of breaking the rhythm of speedier opponents as well as slowing the game down to a more comfortable pace for you.

Movement After Serving
Movement *immediately* after serve is crucial. The basic rules:

Serve	Movement
Low	in to cover net, stay to intercept
High	back to your mid-court
Drive	*stay to crouch-defend*
Flicked	slightly back, defend own court
Flick	back to defend your mid-court watching out for drop shot; occasionally risk going in after hitting one wide to tramlines

The Mental Skills of Serving
Look confident, preparing to serve. Take *your* time, even for fast serve. Concentrate: shuttle, tape, front line. Watch receiver's racket face on hit, and threaten to intercept.

RECEIVING SERVE
It is useful to repeat here:
1. The aim in doubles is to get a "successful attack" at the earliest opportunity.
2. Receiving serve is being in a

Rudy Heriyanto (Indonesia) ducks after low serving whilst Kartono (Indonesia) defends the rush-of-serve to his body on his backhand.

state of "static attack" – this does not mean that it is a state of "successful attack", or that it is simple to convert it into one. You can see from the previous paragraphs that it is quite possible to turn defence into attack when serving.

When receiving service your aim should be to make it impossible for the server to mount an attack without increasing the likelihood of giving away easy points by making short rally errors.

As in singles (see page 19), most unforced errors come from the second stroke of the rally, though for somewhat different reasons. Firstly, the ability to make a varied number of quick-decision returns, especially in reply to a low serve, involves a highly-co-ordinated technique. Second, and more importantly, the receiver feels under pressure (particularly in mens' doubles) to create a "winning attack" and is thus tempted to make the return of serve too aggressive.

You need to consider the following points when attempting to make a successful attack whilst avoiding the pitfalls of too much aggression:

1. *Receiving stance.* This is similar to the backward-attacking stance (see lower photo page 25).
2. *Receiving position* (Diags. 9 and 10, pages 33 and 34).
3. *Server's normal services* (see page 34).
4. *Type of serve* (see page 40).
5. *Server's position* (page 38) *and next movement.* Would a hairpin net-shot be a safe reply?
6. *Server's partner's position and*

stance. If attacking his body, to which side?

The best way of developing a successful attack when receiving is to play a first shot that might win the rally but which is intended as a set-up for you to end the rally on *your second shot* (or your partner's first shot).

Thus your receiving-serve policy

should be committed to a relatively
error-free successful attack which
concentrates on the winning of a
receiving rally on the *fourth* stroke.

Finally, in order to ensure a good
chance of continuing this successful
attack, you should be clear as to
what is going to be *your* next movement after receiving serve.

In general, unless you give away

Mike Tredgett (England) takes
advantage of his left hand to net-
intercept, thereby protecting Ray
Stevens' (England) backhand.

the static attack with a lob or a clear,
you should stay forward to attack net
replies *and* intercept any other shots
within your reach.

Level Doubles II: Attack and Defence

PAIRING-UP

Traditionally, badminton has been regarded as an individual sport, but level doubles is a team game and should be thought of as such by both partners. Any team game revolves around the individual technical and tactical ability of each player blended to create a successful team performance – badminton level doubles is no exception to this.

Here is an example of technical and tactical "partnership blending" via an analysis of a hypothetical player's level doubles strengths and weaknesses as follows:

1. Somewhat inconsistent low serve but a large variety of deceptive serves. These result in either hard "rushes" at partner or surprised flick lobs or clears relinquishing the static attack.

2. Fast around net area with aggressive anticipation for forecourt interceptions.

3. Consistent in turning defence into attack by returning smashes low and straight past net attacker into mid-court area.

An individual analysis of this player's *ideal* level doubles partner's strengths and weaknesses would be: consistent low serve; heavy smash; prefers to be at the back because he is slow moving sideways across the forecourt, but has keen anticipation when the shuttle is low in opponents' mid-court; is fast moving forward with relatively error-free net knock-offs when coming into the **T** (Diags. 21 and 21a).

When deciding on a partner, one of the most important considerations

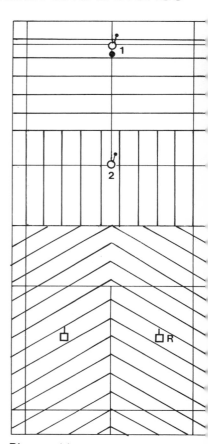

Diagram 14

⧄ differently shaded areas represent individual player's responsibility. Both defenders stand straight-on; as ⧄ is slightly across from shuttle, he should defend any shot going down middle. (NB *cross-defender takes the middle.*)

(Right) Sun Zian goes in to cover the forecourt as Yao Ximing jump-smashes a flick serve.

is that you should be able to communicate freely and easily with each other. It is not necessary to be close friends and, in fact, if the relationship is very close, it can be a hindrance. Partners' styles of play need to be complementary; recognition of each other's strengths and weaknesses and willingness to adjust individual play accordingly are essential. There are bound to be occasions when one or both of you are having a bad day, so it is vital that you are able to encourage each other as well as offer practical support and advice.

ATTACK AND DEFENCE

The simplest attack and defence formations are shown in Diag. 14. The way these formations are changed by subtle alterations in shuttle depths and heights are shown in Diags. 15 and 15a.

Doubles positional play is dictated by the shuttle angle. We have already looked at the movements following various serving and receiving tactics (see pages 43 and 45). The basic in-rally tactics are set out below:

It can sometimes be a winning tactic to concentrate on defending when there are slow shuttles, your opponents have weak smashes, are unfit or, dislike a slow pace.

Ladies' doubles should be a game of defence leading to counter attack. Unless the opposing pair make an outright loser in reply to your defence, however, there is a point during every rally where, in order to win it, you *have* to attack.

TURNING DEFENCE INTO ATTACK

You can turn defence into attack by either just taking a calculated risk going into the net or by changing the current pattern of shuttle angles.

Straight-on Defence

As a straight-on defender, you can:
1. Crouch-defend (Diags. 17 and 17a) unless previous clear or lob is short.
2. Straight-lob deeper, then crouch-defend.
3. Cross-lob, then move towards **T** as an "attacking" cross-defender.
4. Straight drive or push past net attacker, then take up backward attacking stance nearer net.

Basic In-Rally Movements

Shuttle angle	Your position/ stance	Shuttle angle	Your position/ stance
High to you	move back to attack at rear.	High straight	defend straight-on, mid-court.
High to partner	move in to attack net or forecourt.	High cross-court	also defend middle.
High to opponent	defend own mid-court.	Flat either side	crouch-defend/ attack stance.

Mixed serving positions and stances demonstrated by two English All-England champions, Gillian Gilks and Martin Dew.

Thomas Kihlstrom (Sweden) hits powerfully and high with graceful ease deep out of his backhand corner.

Gymnastic English National champion Helen Troke lunges at full stretch for a wide, low forehand block.

The balletic athleticism of a mid-air jump smash is magnificently displayed here by Sun Zhian (China).

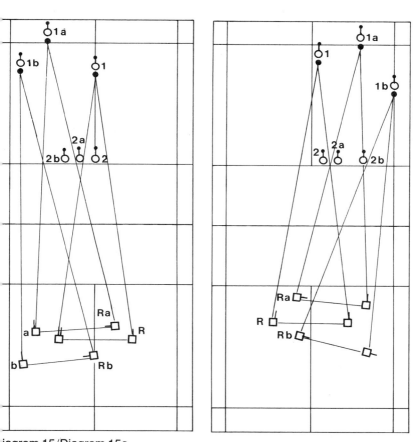

Diagram 15/Diagram 15a

Cross-defender stands closer to net than straight-defender to be equidistant from shuttle. Isosceles triangle "tilts" with shuttles hit from varying depths and angles.

Cross-drive or push past net attacker, then take up forward attacking stance near **T**.

Cross-block.

Straight-block very tight to tape.

The last two options are more effective in reply to "outside" smashing when the net attacker may be further back, (Diag. 18) or when a pair often use this formation.

Cross-Defence

As cross-defender, you should be aware of your role in the isosceles triangle and ensure that you are always at least slightly in front of your partner. You can: move across further to take the "inside" smash as well as the one down the middle (Diag. 20a); crouch-defend straight-on to shuttle; drive, push or lob *away* straight from both attackers so that your partner could become an attacking cross-defender; threaten the back attacker by constantly hunting for the shuttle, looking out especially for his drop shots, but obviously wanting to get involved in the rally by taking calculated risks.

MAINTAINING THE ATTACK

You can maintain the attack by:

1. "Inside" straight-smashing, thereby reducing the angle of reply, because it is then difficult for the straight-defender to play a cross-court (Diags. 16 and 16a);

2. Judicious use of fast clears, especially against a pair who, as attacking cross-defenders, like to creep forward close to the **T** (Diags. 17/17a);

3. Using drop shots or pushes midway *between* the defenders – this latter tactic is the safest method

and often produces a winner b causing indecision (Diags. 19/19a);

4. Directed driving downwards to wards the backhand side of eithe defender when they are in a crouc stance.

General Points

In ladies' doubles unless you ar very long in the leg or slow gettin back for fast clears, use crouch defence, taking advantage smashes (slower in level double than in mixed) by moving up th court.

In men's doubles (although partly applies to ladies), remembe that your opponents, like you, *are an attacking formation at the begi ning of every rally* and this is crucial time, therefore, to be goin for winners. After the third or four strokes of each rally, a definite pa tern of attack and defence evolve (at least temporarily), and the ear winning chance is then lost.

It is incredibly difficult to retur smashes or attacking net shots awa from the net attacker when they ar hit straight at the body. When doubt, net attackers, push or tap th shuttle directly *at* the defender chest until you get a reply that yc can more safely knock-off.

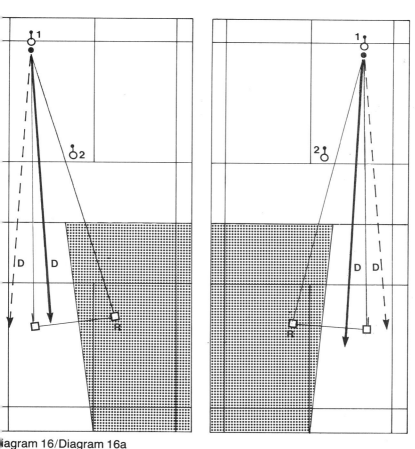

Diagram 16/Diagram 16a

◻ Straight defender will be straight-on *or* cover his tramline area, whilst ◻ **R** cross-defender will bias his defensive stance to cover middle area of court. —► Smash "outside", easy to cross-court, ➤ smash "inside", difficult to cross-court. ▦ Shaded area is tactical responsibility of ◻ **R** cross-defender. (B *cross-defender takes the middle* – smash, drop, drive or clear.)

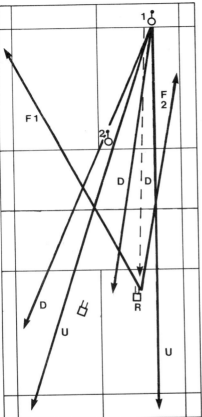

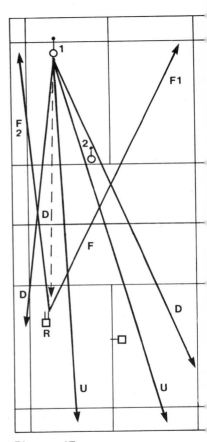

Diagram 17

 R moves up and left to crouch-defend; turned to shuttle, crouch-defends; **O2** seeing crouch-defender, should move back right of **T** to intercept Stroke 1; **O1** counters crouch-defence with straight or cross-court clear, steep smash to left hip of crouch-defender, or hard smash cross-court, wrong siding cross-defender.

Diagram 17a

□ **R** moves up and left to crouch-defend; □ moves left, backhand-defending gap. **O2** seeing crouch-defender, should move back left of **T** to intercept F1; **O1** counters crouch defence with straight or cross-court clear, steep smash to left hip of crouch-defender or hard smash cross-court, wrong siding cross-defender.

Level Doubles III: Specific Teamwork

Once you have paired up with a partner with whom your style of play makes a satisfactory blend you can develop your own team tactics. You should now be discussing, particularly off-court, the three areas of your team game:

1. On-court decisons that may need to be made, especially regarding the Laws.

2. Methods to be used for serve and receive or attack and defence. This will depend upon your individual strengths and weaknesses. On a similar basis, what tactics, specific to either of you will be used.

3. Opponent analysis: general match strategy and specific game situations that you wish to regularly set up (see page 26).

ON-COURT DECISIONS

The start of each game is important so thought must be given not only to which side serves first, but which partner serves or receives first. Ability, preparedness, preference for either half of the court (at game or match points, particularly) will need to be considered. For example, if one of you has just had a long run of serves winning the first or second game, it may be advisable to serve first in the next game regardless of previous plans.

In such situations it is essential (and polite) to inform your opponents and the umpire if there is a change in the court from which you are starting. This will avoid confusion and arguments about the score. The following should clarify the fault rules about serving or receiving

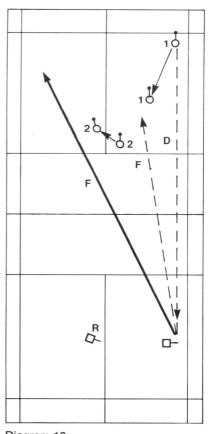

Diagram 18
Defending in level doubles against "outside" straight-smashing.
O1 smashes to ☐ defender on forehand; O2 moves to intercept Stroke F1. O1 moves to cover stroke F2.

from the wrong service court.

1. If the fault is not discovered *before* the next rally begins, then

the score stands and the players do not change back to their correct positions.

2. If the pair at fault *lose* the rally, the players do not change back to their correct positions, and the fault stands.

3. If the pair at fault *win* the rally, the players change back to their correct positions, and play a let.

4. If *both* pairs are at fault, however, the players change back and play a let *regardless* of the outcome of the rally.

Such an occurrence can usually be avoided by ensuring that one of your pair clearly calls both score and service after each rally.

The end of each game is equally or more important than the beginning so you need to consider the choices at 13–13 and 14–14. These are even more subtle than in singles (see page 31).

Mathematically speaking, in doubles you will have the following chance of success, assuming a 50% success rate for both pairs and all players when serving:

You will see that when there seems to be nothing to sway your choice, your best option is to choose to set. Obviously, some of the same factors as in singles apply here, but much more depends on which players within each pair are serving and receiving and exactly how the serve-receive situation has been developing between the individual contestants throughout the game.

PARTNERSHIP METHODS

So far you have seen *three* main positional situations in level doubles: *serve-receive*, *attack* and *defence*. There is, however, a *fourth*, which is that "grey area" where both pairs, in crouch or backward/forward attacking stances, are *jostling for the attack* with drives or pushes from and to mid-court and/or at each other's body.

Exactly what tactical methods you use in these four situations needs to be carefully examined by taking into account two more areas of your team game partnership effectiveness and opponent analysis.

SCORE	SERVE CHOICE		YOUR % WINNING	YOUR % LOSING
13–13	1st	Play to 15	49	51
		Set to 5	50	50
13–13	2nd	Play to 15	32	68
		Set to 5	42	58
14–14	1st	Play to 15	40	60
		Set to 3	50	50
14–14	2nd	Play to 15	20	80
		Set to 3	36	64

Partnership Effectiveness

Here are some examples of the considerations involved within each of the four main positional situations. Say your partner is slow moving across net or back-court, has a heavy smash and is strong, hitting out of either corner, but does not like to be attacked fast at his body:

1. *Serve and receive*

Low serve so that it is not easily rushed down the middle ie wider to the tramlines or middle of service court – or even to a point along the line that proves difficult for the specific receiver; *flick serve* high and wide, to allow more time for your partner to prepare for the straight attack. *Receive* using mainly mid-court placements or hairpin net shots, so as to make a defensive lob the most likely reply.

Misbun Sidek (smashing) and Rajiv Sidek go for a match-point attack.

If your partner is left-handed, serving low, wide to the tramlines in the right-hand court will encourage straight replies to his forehand.

2. *Attack*

Net attack The replies to your partner's heavy smash are likely to be weakish blocks to the net or fast drive/flicks, so you should stand well back behind front service line; *smash* – steep, mainly "inside-straight"; *drop shot* – slow and close to net; *drive* and *fast clear* – rarely.

3. *Defence*

You will be a fast mover, especially forward into and around the net and a keen forecourt player. You should defend mainly using cross-court replies, whilst your partner should

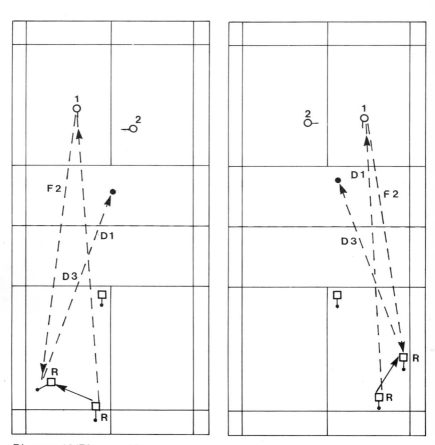

Diagram 19/Diagram 19a

(Stroke 1) ☐ smashes to body of O **1** who (Stroke 2) drives, flicks or pushes past ☐ to mid-court tramlines; (Stroke 3) avoids a "hacking-type" rally starting if loopy upward flicks or flat drives were used, against which ☐ moving back, would be badly positioned to take any subsequent attacking replies.

defend mainly straight and flat to mid-court or back-court, both allowing *you* a chance of becoming an attacking cross-defender. Neither of you would be advised to block-defend to the net.

4. *Jostling for the Attack*

You are the partner who is going to have to do most of this (!), eventually moving forward to attack the net; your greater speed, and superior forecourt effectiveness makes you the creator of winning moves in the partnership. You are the risk-taker, but also the set-up man for your partner's heavier smash. Both of you should try to ensure that the shuttle is coming back fast and flat only when *you* are able to intercept it. When *you* are doubtful of gaining the initiative of a net attack, favour the hairpin net-shot, or a very tight net-block which you can follow in, so as to at least get the advantage of a back-attack from the subsequent high lob to your heavy-smashing partner.

Already mentioned is that the *serving-receiving formations are like jostling for the attack.* It is worth examining the four separate roles.

1. *The server* should be aware of the receiver's likely replies to any low serve so that he can be ready to intercept. If he thinks that receiver is unlikely to rush a particular serve, he should stay upright so as to have a better chance of intercepting. If the receiver rushes, the server should sway his body sideways to let his partner have a clearer view and more hitting space.

He should also be aware of the receiver's likely replies to any de-ceptive flick so that he can decide whether to go into an attacking or defensive position immediately. Basically the server should stay in if his flick has gone behind the receiver or if that opponent's normal reply is a drop shot. In event of a fast, flat flick (which often happens with backhand serving) it is essential for the server to duck in a low crouch-defence at the **T**. If the receiver cross-smashes back at him as he retreats fast to defend at mid-court, it will probably hit him in the chest; if the receiver uses a straight drop shot, the server's partner will not have time to get in for it; a weak drop shot is a likely reply generally and many receivers play this stereo-typed safety shot.

2. The closer the *server's partner* stands behind server the more attacking the tactic, but the more vulnerable the partnership is to a rush of serve. Much will depend on how close to their respective front service lines receiver and server stand, but if the receiver is rushing hard especially down the middle (possibly the server may need to serve from further back, of course) the server's partner will need to adjust his defensive stance backwards. He should be aware of the different positions that server may go into in order to take his calculated-risk-interceptions, at once adopting a "balancing" attack and defence position.

3. Developing a "successful attack" from the "static attack" of receiving was mentioned earlier with regard to *the receiver* (pages 44/45). It is always worth repeating, however,

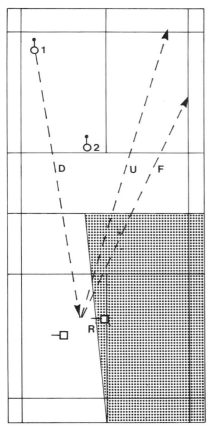

Diagram 20
Cross-defender takes the "inside" smash; straight-defender would follow in cross-lob reply ○**1**, whilst cross-defender would follow in cross-drive or push replies ○**2**.

(Left) The Sidek brothers (Malaysia) both use the centre-court jump in a perfect straight-on defence.

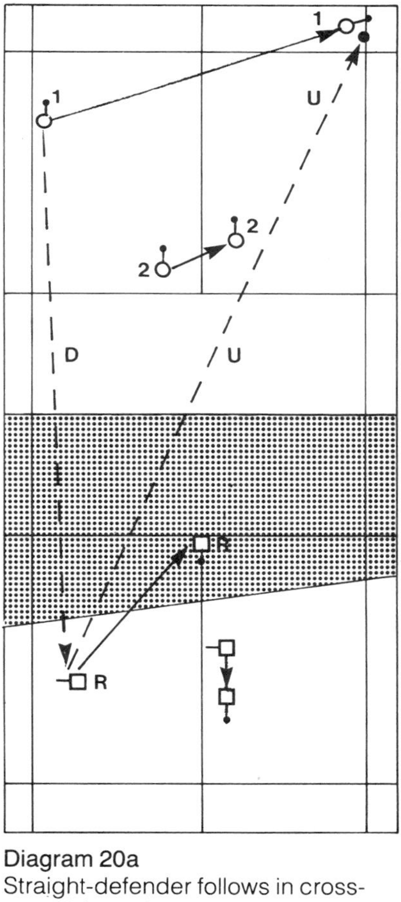

Diagram 20a
Straight-defender follows in cross-court-lob-reply to smash, attacking net area.

that the receiver, unless he lifts the low serve high, should stay on the front line with his racket up, regardless of the receiving policy of trying to gain a "successful attack". He should be prepared to kill any loose low serve.

The receiver's partner should also keep in mind the aim of winning a receiving rally on the *fourth shot* because of the opponents' early semi-defensive strokes (despite their attacking formation). He should be ready to make a sudden counter-attack especially against the fast shots which come past his partner.

Equally important is that on *anything* other than a low serve, he should move in very fast to attack the net without waiting to see if the receiver hits down. Following a flick serve ideally he should be in the net attack stance a metre or so behind the front service line *before* the receiver hits the shuttle. If the receiver happens to clear, then his partner should retreat from net to defend his mid-court area.

Playing with a Weaker Partner

It is possible to develop tactics for playing successfully with a weaker partner. Below is a summary of the methods *both* of you could use:

Stronger Partner

1. *Serving:* drive or flicked, towards the middle line in both courts, so as to make it difficult for receiver to attack other than down similar shuttle pathway; low serve, less frequently, but wide mainly so that you can have a better chance of straight net interceptions.

2. *Receiving:* stand closer to front service line to encourage flicks; take more risks attacking low serves.

3. *Attacking:* drop shots midway between defenders; very hard smashes in varied directions; take more risks.

4. *Defending:* straight and flat drives and pushes or hard cross-courts (all of which you can follow in as net attacker); if you have to lob or clear, make sure it is always straight; no blocking to net area, from where net attacker can hit at your partner's body.

5. *General:* be ultra-positive; take more risks.

Weaker Partner

1. *Serving:* low, with plenty of margin for error as partner must be given the chance of returning the attempted kill of a loose serve; if necessary to flick serve, always wide to tramlines, encouraging straight smash at partner.

2. *Receiving:* preferably hairpin net shot to low serve or *cross-court* lob and stay in, kill loose ones; when possible "inside" straight smash high/flicks, otherwise try to clear cross-court.

3. *Attacking:* drop shots, only when you have to and preferably faster ones midway between defenders; "inside" straight smashes, mainly.

4. *Defending:* straight or cross-court flat drives and pushes, *past* net attacker, and follow in; cross-block and follow in; if you have to lob or clear, make sure it is always cross-court.

5. *General:* allow plenty of margin for error; get into net as soon as possible.

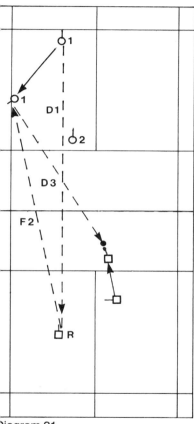

Diagram 21
Back-attacker moves to mid-court for straight-defender's *low* reply to smash; cross-defender moves forward to knock-off.

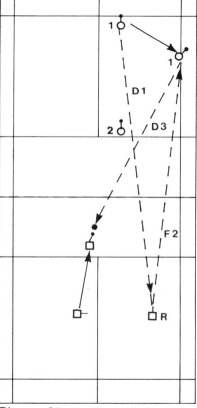

Diagram 21a
Back-attacker moves to mid-court for straight-defender's *flat* reply to smash; cross-defender moves forward to knock-off.

OPPONENT-PAIR ANALYSIS

As with singles (page 26), the most important feature in planning a match strategy in level doubles is to decide how particular opponent pairs' strengths and weaknesses are going to affect the way your partner and yourself play. Generally speaking, even more in doubles than in singles, *it is a dangerous tactic to*

Misbun Sidek forehand defends, whilst Rajiv Sidek crouch-defends the middle backhand.

alter your own game too drastically to cater for specific opponents.

For example, if you are playin against a very uneven standard pa and you try to concentrate your pla on the weaker player only, you ma find yourselves making stroke c positional errors because of this al normal emphasis on one opponent

(a) High or flick serve to weaker partner.
(b) Low serve mainly wide to stronger partner.
(c) If the weak player is at the back, defend high.
(d) If the strong player is at the back; net-defend.
(e) If the strong player is in fore-court, hit high.
(f) Attack weak player's body.

Partners should discuss each match beforehand and decide if it entails adjustments in their personal effectiveness methods, and whether or not any of them, *having regard for the potential hazards of adjusting*, are really worthwhile.

Ruth Damayanti (Indonesia) crouch-defends as Wiharjo Verawaty (Indonesia) defends the middle on her backhand.

Nevertheless, your *general strategy* (as to how you want rallies to progress) would be to hit shuttle somewhere towards weaker player whenever in doubt during a rally. *Specific situations* which you may wish to set up could be as follows:

Mixed Doubles I: Male/Female Roles

Of all the five events available, mixed doubles is tactically the most challenging for both men and women and therefore very stimulating once the overall strategy and individual demands are understood by both partners.

At the end of the previous section the tactics to be used against an uneven standard pair and the problems of playing within a similar type of partnership at level doubles were examined. In many ways mixed doubles provides the ultimate answer to uneven-pair tactics.

The basic strategy is centred around the fact that the woman is the weaker player and as such she should take care of that part of the court where she is most effective ie, the net area and forecourt, whilst the stronger man adopts a centre-court position looking after the mid-court and back-court. This does *not* mean that it is a game of men's singles with the lady sometimes getting in the way(!) In fact the lady should usually look and be the more dynamic member of the team, with the man making openings for her.

Having adopted this *attacking "front and back" formation*, each pair then must constantly play the strokes best suited to maintain (or reverse) the static attack and to develop it into a successful attack. This has to be done far more subtly than in level doubles. Thus mixed doubles creates constant "cat and mouse" mid-court situations with both pairs in attacking formations manoeuvring the opponents out of position either over to one side of court in order to go for cross-court

or cross-net winners, or up and down both sides of court so that woman can intercept (Diags. 28 28a).

The strokes best suited to keep the attack (unless the shuttle is already high on your side) are those that make the shuttle travel fast and low ie drives, blocks and pushes to mid-court and net area, together with attacking and defensive net shots.

In comparison with a woman, a man has greater explosive power, hitting strength and moving speed. On a badminton court this means he can accelerate, move, stop and change direction more effectively, hit the shuttle harder and take it earlier – all important factors in putting pressure on opponents and in hitting winners. These "sex advantages" have no bearing whatsoever on the most important stroke in doubles – the service. Nor indeed is there any difference between the sexes in touch-play, creativity or cunning.

Realizing this, the lady should spend much of her practice time on cultivating an *accurate* low serve (not necessarily as varied as suggested for level doubles), with a deceptive flick serve to all corners. She should also *take risks, especially net interceptions.*

It has been my experience and it certainly still seems to be the case at club level – that the woman partner is actively discouraged from really

Martin Dew (England) moves across to take an early forehand drive in mid court.

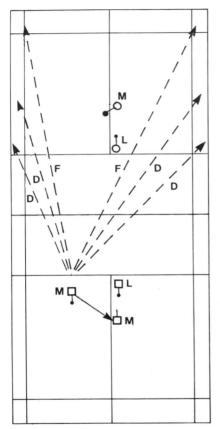

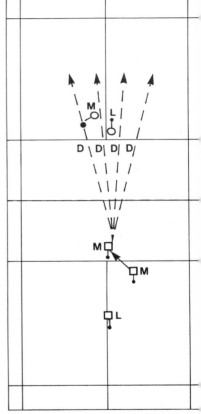

Diagram 22

□ L is weaker player, except at net, so
□ M receives from further back and will
try to play attacking placement shots
to back and side tramlines to give him
time to recover back to mid-court;
OL stands slightly across T, legs wide
and leaning over to her left so that
OM can serve anywhere along service
line (even using a forehand serving
action).

Diagram 23

□ L is accomplished all-court player,
so □ M takes up more attacking positi
and will try to "rush" serve *towards
middle* then "smother" any replies to
net area; OL stands on T, legs wide
and leaning well over to her left so th
OM can serve anywhere along servic
line (even using a forehand service
action).

getting involved in a game of mixed doubles. Unless she is considered to be comparatively better than her male partner, he generally still expects her to "low serve perfectly then duck out of the rally". Until, that is, it is necessary for her to kill an "easy" net knock-off or intercept, from the opposing man, the inevitable cross-court drive which he was too slow to cover!

Badminton mixed doubles is an exceptional sports event since the Laws are such that, unlike other mixed games, there is no way the weaker woman player can be forced to the back of the court. Only once every few rallies, when receiving serve, can she be pushed back from the relative safety of the net.

Tactically and technically speaking, it can be very dangerous for opponents to endeavour to concentrate their play on the opposing lady. Hitting to the net area and forecourt risks shots going into the net whilst strokes to the forecourt open up many easy winning possibilities for the opposition.

The major difference between the various levels of mixed doubles play is the *commitment* of the lady. The better at mixed she is, the more she will commit herself to the straight shots when attacking and the cross-court shots when defending. In mixed, to a greater extent than in level doubles, *each pair should adopt an attacking formation when defending* (Diags. 28, 28a, 30).

The man, whilst giving his partner full rein to go for interceptions, should shadow all her movements so that he can take the shots she fails to cut off or reach.

Having now established quite clearly the *positional roles* of the partnership which dictate the winning tactics, it follows that the *general strategy is to try to reverse these roles in opposing partnerships*, by enticing the lady into the mid- and back-court areas and the man into the net and forecourt areas.

Mixed Doubles II: Specific Teamwork

Now that the separate roles have been defined – basically that of woman as net attacker and man as back attacker – the next stage is to examine how these roles complement each other, and how these roles in the opposing pair can be reversed.

SERVE AND RECEIVE
Man Receiving

The relative strength of his partner should dictate, to a large extent, the man's receiving tactics (see Diags. 22 and 23). If the man wants his partner to stand near the **T**, his receiving stance should be further back; he is unable to commit himself to attack the low serve because, unless it is a very poor delivery, he can never guarantee a kill. He should, therefore, play a flat pushed or flicked reply to the forecourt, mid-court or back-court sides and move back quickly to a central position leaving his partner to cover all return shots to the forecourt.

Although this tactic means giving away much of the static attack, it allows him to initiate a successful attack by astute placements into areas away from and/or in between the serving partnership (Diag. 22). The fact that he is standing further back should eliminate most of the danger of being flick served, unless of course he jumps forward too early to try to "rush" serve.

If he is flick served, the ideal reply is a *steep* smash to give his partner a better chance to intercept the *straight* defensive reply, with the shuttle coming up rather than flat. Effective alternative replies are

drop shots down the sides, preferably straight, or a fast cross-court clear.

If his partner is skilful and confident in the mid- and back-court – ie if she plays a reasonably effective all-court level doubles – the man should stand close to the front service line, assuming he is athletic and quick enough to get back for any flicks, and go for a "rush and smother" policy (Diag. 23). As in men's doubles, he should attack the low serve hard back towards the middle (or kill the loose one, preferably towards the sides) in order to force a block to the net or a flat reply, both of which *he* should intercept. In this way, he will be adopting the same receiving tactics as in level doubles – developing a successful attack by setting up a receiving rally so that there is less chance of his making an error on the second stroke and most chance of a winner (usually by him) on the *fourth* stroke of the rally. Meanwhile his partner should watch his movements after receiving, deciding if he is staying in to "smother". If he makes a placement shot, he will come back quickly to his central position (as in Diag. 22) and she should move quickly into net area.

Lady Receiving

As was mentioned earlier, this is the one time when the opposition can *force* the lady away from the front, attempting to get a weak reply and/or reverse the front and back roles, so it is a particularly significant situation in mixed doubles tactics.

The *low serve* should be received

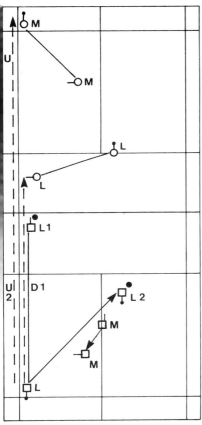

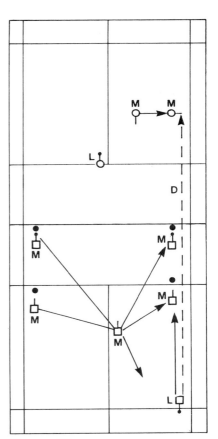

Diagram 24

□ L moves straight in for net-shot reply to her straight drop shot or across and in for cross-court attack to her clear; □ M moves back and across for straight smash or clear into his backhand; O L stands left of T, legs wide, racket-up, narrows angle for any cross-court attack whilst watching out for straight drop shot; O M expects straight smash, then moves back hoping for winner with own straight smash.

Diagram 25

□ L following in half-smash, must not be tempted *back* for a second overhead shot; □ M "ready" to move back for lifted replies but also to take any blocks to help □ L out of trouble, or even possibly to play a surprise knock-off winner; O L stands right of T, legs wide, racket up, narrows angle for any cross-court attack whilst watching out for straight drop shot; O M expects straight smash, then stretches to reach the half-smash on his backhand.

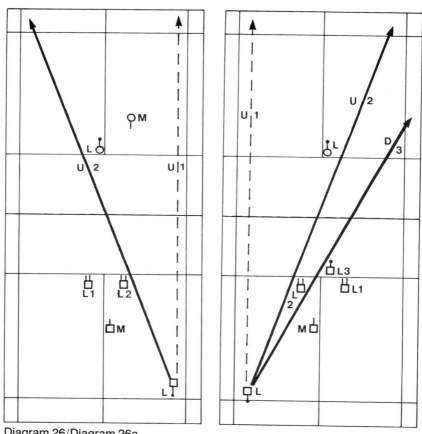

Diagram 26/Diagram 26a

Straight clears, whilst easier to play, make ☐**L** run to ☐**L1** so as to cover
○**M** cross-court attack – this is further than ☐**L2** and would entail her going
across her partner's line of vision. Fast cross-court clears (➤) are the most
effective counter-tactic, as they are well *away* from both opponents,
allowing ☐**M** and ☐**L** time to get into position, yet still being potential winners.
Cross-court smashes (or even drop shots ➤) are best attempted only towards
the backhand side of opponents.

in similar fashion to the man who
stands slightly further back to receive, (Diag. 22). As she stands like
this to *discourage flick serves*, it is
unlikely that she will be quick

enough to attack a good low serve.
The *flick serve* should be received in such a way that she has
time to get back into the net.
Diag. 25 shows perhaps the ideal

reply, which is a half-smash straight, making opposing man stretch across and slightly forward. Although she will want to follow in quickly, her helpful partner must be prepared (taking up a slightly more forward central position) to move in fast either to help his partner, if she cannot get there quickly enough (for instance, if her smash were too hard) or to attack, if he feels the opposing man is going to block.

Diag. 24 shows two alternative replies: a *straight drop shot*, which is a very safe reply, so long as opposing lady is covering the cross-court attack; a *straight clear*, even if high, is just about the worst reply – unless fast into backhand corner – as it draws opposing man's attack on to her as he follows in, having to run *across* her own man's line of vision as she attempts to cover the cross-court attack in crouch defence.

As with the *high serve* (although the increased time the shuttle is in the air makes it easier), a punched clear cross-court may surprise the opposition and will allow her to be well placed for any cross-court attack (Diags. 26/26a). If she wants to reply with a cross-court drop or smash, it is advisable to do so only to the opposing lady's backhand side (Diag. 26a).

Man Serving

The man should usually serve from mid-court (especially to a man receiving near the front service line, in order to be able to better return any "rush") so as to keep control of the rear court. Whilst this results in a flatter trajectory low serve and a

central ready position for an attacking reply to his flick serve, it nevertheless gives receiver more time to see any serve variations.

His partner should position herself a few inches behind the **T** depending upon her serving partner's position, racket up, legs wide and leaning to her left so that he can direct his low serve *anywhere* along the front service line.

His serving attitude will differ with the two receivers:

1. *To the man:* he will concentrate on *defence* with a variety of low serves to bring him forward, but still be able to underarm flick-clear all the subsequent replies. Occasional flick serves should be mainly down the middle if he wants to have the best chance of getting the smash back himself, or wide if his partner is good at crouch defending against cross-court smashes, in which case he can reasonably commit himself to going for the straight.

2. *To the lady:* he will concentrate on *attack*, with a larger variety of all serves, especially flicks and high, to push her back.

Lady Serving

The conflict created by an aggressive male receiver trying to "psyche out" a female server often dominates a mixed match. She should usually serve from close up to the front service line, so as to give him less time to attack either low or flick serves, and to be able to threaten any net returns.

The male partner should position himself roughly in the centre-court, though this will vary depending

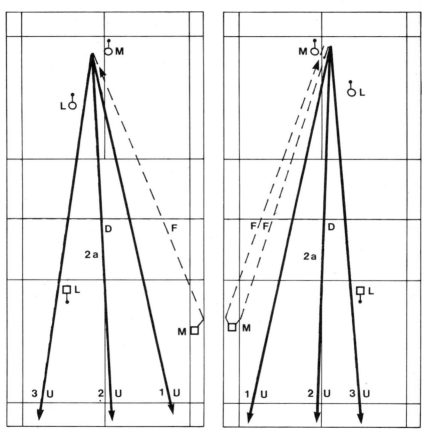

Diagram 27/ Diagram 27a

☐ **L** stands racket-up a metre behind front service line prepared for straight short clear or smash. As shuttle is being received at such an awkward angle (even if she manages to intercept it early) and as ☐ **L** wants to get back into net area, cross-court clear (Stroke 1) is the *simplest* way to neutralize this tactic. Straight clear above backhand side of ☐ **L** (Stroke 3) is the most effective way to gain attack. If ☐**M** stands close (or right up) to front service tramline or follows in aggressively, ☐ **L** should move back slightly – in which case Stroke 1 becomes the ideal counter-tactic.

orten Frost of Denmark moves with classical footwork to play a perfectly
lanced forehand net lob.

An airborne Helen Troke (England) on her way to a leaping backhand lunge net shot.

upon the receiving style of opposing man and woman.

Her serving attitude will also depend upon which opponent she is serving to. She should appreciate that *her ability and confidence in serving to the opposing man will probably be the deciding factor in the final result.*

Whilst having a variety of serves is valuable, only two alternatives are really necessary – a consistently accurate one to the **T** and a deceptive full-length flick. A third, the one wide to either tramline, should be used particularly if opposing man is "rushing" too well into partner's body or the opposing lady receives serve from too far back.

It is following an accurate low serve that a woman can start to dominate the game from the forecourt by anticipating and "leaning in" pushed replies within reach of her racket-up stance.

TACTICS WITHIN THE RALLY
The Attack

So far three main avenues of developing a successful attack into a rally-winning situation in mixed doubles have been explored. These are all at the *serve-receive stage*:

. Reversing the positions of the opponents by serving mainly high to the lady and low to the man.

. Man attacking serve (including flick serves).

. Lady cutting off pushed replies to low serves (including her partner's low serve).

The following are more ways of creating openings for hitting win-

ners later in the rally (Diags. 28, 28a, 29, 30).

1. Whilst both pairs are playing mid-court and sparring for the attack, your lady partner takes risks by making straight net interceptions.

2. Manoeuvre opposing man out of position to one side by playing straight blocks/pushes/fast drops to mid-court tramline area – his partner will be looking for the right moment to go for straight net interceptions, so that it is unlikely that she will be covering your subsequent cross-court drives or flicks.

3. Manoeuvre opposing lady out of position to one side by playing straight blocks/pushes/fast drops to net area – her partner will have to cover too much court to be able to reach your subsequent cross-court pushes or net shots.

4. Manoeuvre *both* opponents out of position to one side of the court by playing straight blocks/pushes/fast drops into the mid-court/forecourt gap between them – then play any shot cross-court, preferably a flick deep.

It is extremely dangerous to risk hitting a cross-court shot until one or both opponents are positioned to one side of court.

5. Hit straight or cross-court drives deep into the corners, then the lady, racket up, positions herself to counter-attack the cross-court drop shots or drives, whilst the man positions himself to cover all straight replies, even a drop shot.

6. Having forced the opposing man back from mid-court with a deep drive or fast clear, or having brought his partner right into net area with a

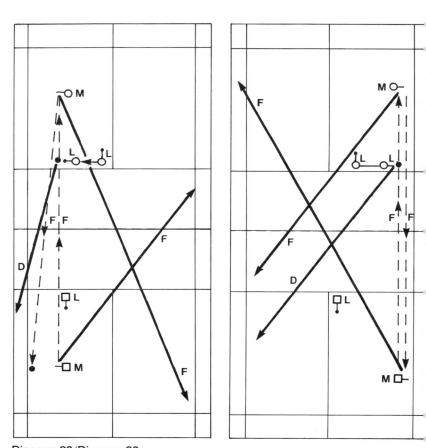

Diagram 28/Diagram 28a
Both pairs try to keep the shuttle low and flat (--→), looking for the opportunity play potential winners (→), particularly cross-court or, for lady to intercept.

close net-skimming push/block, hit into the mid-court/forecourt gap.

. Lift shuttle high and deep into either corner, then the lady, racket up, positions herself to counter-attack the cross-court smash, whilst the man positions himself to cover all straight replies, even a drop shot.

. If smashing cross-court from mid-or rear court, hit to the backhand side of the counter-attacking lady crouch defender.

. As the man attacking from one side mid-court or rear court, against a pair adopting the diagonal defence (see page 51), smash midway between them.

0. As the man (or the lady if you find yourself behind your partner) frequently make use of the *punched clear cross-court* from the back-court.

The Defence

Once the shuttle has been lifted high there are *three* defensive strategies:

. *Front and back defence* is where both players retain a roughly down-the-middle position. The woman crouched low just on the **T**, should not attempt to take any smash, but merely be ready for a drop shot either side, ensuring that she does not block the view of her partner. The man waits centre-court hoping to be able to successfully block the reply.

. *Sides defence* is where the lady moves back cross-court to take up the role of cross-defender. Depending upon the relative standards of the two partners, the lady should only do this when she feels it is a last resort to give a better chance of sustaining the rally. The danger is that, not only does this tactic offer up opportunities for an attack to be directed at the woman (especially a smash across her), but it also presents a chance to force her back with a fast clear.

3. *Diagonal defence* is where the lady crouches a little way behind the front line, cross-court from the shuttle, expecting a smash at her, but watching out for the straight drop shot. She should resist any temptation to move back to take a fast clear.

Whichever defence is adopted, the aim of the lady should be to play a reply (preferably a fast block) mid-court away from the opponents and follow it into the net.

Meeting the shuttle early is probably the most important factor in mixed doubles (after serving well). The man should try to move *forward*, as well as across, when intercepting drives, pushes and underarm flicks. The lady should try to get her attacking/pushing net replies down in front of mid-court to make the opposing man reach in front of him, otherwise she risks her fast flat attack at the man being cross-block-ed too fast for her to reach it.

Serving to the lady from wide in the tramlines is a tactic rarely used and yet it has been used to great effect even in world-class mixed doubles and it is a tactic that is well worth using.

Diags. 27/27a show clearly that Stroke 1 is not only the most realistic reply, but probably also the most practical because the lady receiver would have plenty of time to follow it

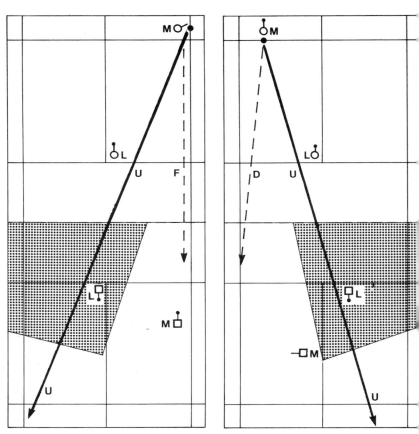

Diagram 29/Diagram 30

▓▓ shaded areas are *tactically* lady's responsibility; –▶ dotted arrows are shots which are *tactically* ☐**M** man's responsibility (Diagram 29 backhand straight push; Diagram 30 forehand straight drop shot) but which ☐ **L** lady should attack if she "reads" them early enough. ▶ are shots which are *tactically* dangerous, but likely winners. (Diagram 29 cross-court backhand sweep; Diagram 30 cross-court punched clear) which are more effective if shuttle pathway is over the *left* side of ○**L** lady opponent, who may be further back in a crouch-defence.

in to become cross-court defender.

One of the main problems this tactic causes for the receiving partnership is that it makes the lady feel that the opposing male server is "sorting her out", exposing her movement and stroke weaknesses and generally "getting on top" by confidently and (very obviously) moving right over to one side of the court at the very start of the rally.

In order to be well-positioned and well-balanced for any of these serves, including such variations as the quickly delivered wide, low serve – the lady should adopt an attacking receiving stance, *straight-on to the shuttle* positioned slightly further over to the middle line.

There may be times when the serve is such a difficult angle that she cannot meet it early (and may even in the right-hand court have to take it on her low backhand) – whatever, she should try to at least hit it *high* past the opposing lady.

It is in this situation particularly, when the female partner feels under pressure (especially from the opposing man), that it is crucial for her partner to give practical advice in a *friendly helpful manner*. It is this attitude that is likely to produce an effective counter to any new strategy but, more importantly, it helps cement the necessary co-operative relationship in a doubles team, especially mixed.

Lene Koppen (Denmark) crouch-defends Billy Gilliland's rush-of-serve whilst Karen Chapman (England – just in picture) covers the mid-court and Steen Skovgaard (Denmark) defends his own mid-court.

Mixed "serve-receive" situation. Nora Perry flick serves wide to Imelda Wigoeno (Indonesia) and covers the cross-court, whilst Mike Tredgett and Hadinata Christian wait poised in the mid-court.

Mixed "cat and mouse" mid-court situation. Nora Perry intercepts straight with Billy Gilliland and Karen Chapman struggling to take shuttle low on their backhand side. Mike Tredgett waits poised in the mid-court.

Mixed "cat and mouse" mid-court situation. Nora Perry hits a cross-court net-shot to out-position Imelda Wigoeno. Both men wait poised in the mid-court centre.

Your Personal Improvement Plan

Having made a personal analysis of your game (see page 13), so that you have a clear picture of where your weak areas are, you should list realistic aims and the plans to achieve them. These should include your short, medium and long term competitive ambitions.

ON-COURT PRACTICE

The way to improve any element of your game is to practise, repeating it regularly and correctly.

Practice does *not* always make perfect, in the sense that we want, however. Practice makes *permanent* that which is practised. Just as correct practice develops correct behaviour, so incorrect practice will develop incorrect behaviour, and it is very often easier (particularly with technique practice) to practise incorrectly.

You should repeat some part of the game that you wish to improve – a tactic in the same way as a technique – in order to get it right. You should continue to do so until you reach the *overlearning* stage, where you carry out the correct movements and actions *without consciously thinking about them* – in scientific terms, it becomes automised motor behaviour which is the "permanent" mentioned above. This is why players of long standing find *changing* an automised tactical move or a technique so difficult and often, under competitive pressure, impossible. Re-learning, ie creating a stronger habit, obviously causes far more problems than completely new learning. Coaches the world over are constantly searching for

improved methods of as we say "teaching an old dog, new tricks".

Most club players used to improve by constant repetition of within-club competitive games against each other. For the inexperienced new club member, learning tactics by trial and error within a competitive game is a dreadfully slow process, and it is often a very frustrating experience for partners and opponents – assuming he still has any by the time he has learnt!

There is considerable benefit from specific in-game *tactical* practice, however, in that it automatically *relates the emphasis on to the opponent* and what is done to him. Nevertheless, the exact situation requiring practice may not occur often enough within a normal game, so it is vital to devise other means of practice which allow a greater but meaningful repetition of the desired new learning.

This is best done by setting up a "drill" (also known as a routine, but this usually refers to a technique practice) where a specific part of a rally is repeated continuously, preferably leading to some sort of winning attack.

Unfortunately, like technical practice, tactical learning cannot be easily transferred directly into normal competitive play.

Firstly, the opponent's responses will not necessarily follow any set pattern which may cause you to revert to your still-strong habit and, secondly, the drill may not fully develop total confidence to use the new skill or try out difficult re-learning.

There are three alternative methods of practising new tactical moves so that they can be *gradually* introduced into tough competitive matches.

1. A *conditioned game* where additional rules ensure an emphasis on the desired practised part;

2. A *friendly game*, where you try to win, but not at the expense of development, ie consistently attempting the desired practised part;

3. A *formal competition* where your main aim is to win, but where the standard of the opposition is such that you can sensibly try out the new tactical move, in a planned fashion, ensuring that when the scores get close, you revert (if necessary) to your more familiar "winning" game.

Final points on practice: it should simulate, as closely as possible, the actual game situation; it should be varied to keep it interesting; it requires discipline and concentration to retain quality; the ideal amount and distribution of practice varies with the individual and the required practice.

MENTAL REHEARSAL

The use of mental imagery can valuably enhance the rate of improvement of technique, tactic or psychologically stressful competitive situation. There are many methods for using one's imagination to rehearse the new tactical learning: the simplest involves about five or so minutes per day relaxing, quietly on your own and "clearing the mind" so as to create a vivid picture of the required practice. In this way a huge amount of "practice"

in a very short space of time is possible by constantly repeating the same picture of yourself making the *correct* tactical move.

You should use this method, and other more practical means on court, to learn to concentrate more intensely, control your emotions and conceal any annoyance, discomfort or tiredness – a loss of personal firmness in any of these areas is guaranteed to encourage an astute opponent.

To obtain the best results you should intersperse these imagery sessions with "real thing" in actual practice or competition.

ATTENTION TO DETAIL

Interestingly enough, this is a factor which links champions from all sorts of fields. It involves planning fastidiously to ensure the best chance of victory, arranging such things as a higher carbohydrate diet just before and during competition, ensuring that all equipment is suitable for the conditions and for your mood, with plenty of spares, a comprehensive personal sports first-aid kit – and a copy of the Laws in your holdall!

HEALTH AND FITNESS

Badminton is a very physically demanding game and whilst it is quite normal to be healthy but unfit, it is impossible to be fully fit, if unhealthy.

The ideal way to keep healthy is to ensure, as far as possible, that you *keep a balance in life*. In order to fulfill an ambition, it helps to be single-minded, but the ambition itself must be put into the correct perspective. For example, to lose a particular match may seem like the end of the world to you, but you can be certain that the sun will still rise the next day.

Seriously though, your diet alone can dictate your healthiness and whilst the average person suffers from much of the modern diet of junk foods, additives and monosodium glutomates, a sports person cannot perform with maximum efficiency without a balanced diet, in particular fresh fruit, green vegetables and bran fibres.

A little and often applies to most balancing in life but especially to regular eating, digesting – and waste disposal. Energy for sport is more effectively obtained from carbohydrates than fats or proteins.

Rest, relaxation and entertainment are essential to health and without recuperation after training or hard play, the body will *not* adapt and get fitter, generally or specifically.

Fitness for badminton is best achieved by regular physically-demanding and varied practice sessions, two or three times per week as a minimum.

A firm base of core cardiosvascular fitness can be acquired by other activities like middle distance running, swimming, skipping, but if these methods are used they must be treated as *alternatives* to more specific court movement work, and must never be contemplated other than as an out of season variation.

Until recently, there was a trend for fitness training to be almost totally concentrated on the improvement of muscular strength and heart/lung efficiency. Fortunately, the latest craze for various types of dance (including aerobics and popmobility) has given rise to a greater awareness of the need for *flexibility*.

Ten minutes per day spent on stretching (quite passively) the achilles, calves, hamstrings, quadriceps, hip, shoulder and back areas will prove more effective, in badminton fitness terms, than any other form of training. A further bonus is that this will *help prevent injury*, the worst enemy of fitness.

Sports injuries should be treated *immediately* (and a professional consulted within two days, if possible). The result of a sports injury can be external and/or internal. For general minor injuries, small cuts and local swellings for instance, the basic treatment is to stop playing and reduce the swelling by a cold application, and if it is a limb injury (which is frequently the case), it should be elevated. In *all* instances, stop and rest.

Thus, RICE (another useful mnemonic):

Rest (ie stop and sit/lie down)
Ice (or other cold application)
Compression (a firm local bandage)
Elevation (in the case of limbs).

After 48 hours, you should gradually increase the activity of the injured area, but only within the limits of pain. After four or five days you should gently stretch the injured area until you can obtain the full range of movement, then you may continue with a programme of graduated training leading up to any further competition.

STUDYING AND LEARNING

Observation of better players, especially their tactical moves, rather than just watching for enjoyment, should not be underestimated. Looking carefully at top class performers' tactical style of play (and particularly their techniques) on video, in photos or in the flesh can be invaluable for self-comparison.

Intelligent and enthusiastic players keep an open mind to new ideas and benefit considerably from discussing with colleagues their play, other performers and the game generally.

The quickest and most effective single way to learn, however, is to critically analyse your play with a *coach* who has been confidently recommended by someone whose judgement you trust – the sort of coach who can translate *his* teaching knowledge and playing experience into practical advice in *your* language.

Glossary of Badminton Terms

Aggressive high serve one falling *vertically* near singles back line (useful tactic sometimes in doubles).

Attacking net-shot hit downwards from net area.

Attacking stances poised on balls of feet, legs wide with knees slightly bent, in forecourt with racket up.
(a) *forward* – right foot forward ready to attack in forecourt or net area.
(b) *backward* – left foot forward ready to attack in mid-court or back-court.

Block soft return of smash (or drive) to net area, or further into court.

Checked-smash fast action is checked abruptly before impact, deceptively becoming softly pushed steep drop shot.

Clear high overhead forehand shot.

Clonk backhand attacking net shot, short rebound action, no follow-through.

Crouch-defence standing nearer to net straight-on, racket up in front of face ready to defend either side.

Cue signal given of player's next shot by shuttle position in court and in relation to body stance and movement.

Defensive net-shot hit upwards *from and to* close net area.

Drive smash-action striking shuttle from wide of body; it flies to mid or back horizontally skimming net.

Drive-clear as above, but shuttle flies high to back-court.

Drive-serve hit hard horizontally with fast action of whole arm from the beginning (back) of backswing.

Drop shot *overhead forehand* hit softly, shuttle lands between net and front service line.

Flicked serve hard at a loopy angle just above the receiver's outstretched racket with quick action of hand from beginning/*back* of backswing.

Flick serve as above, but from end/*front* of backswing (ie later flick, more deceptive).

Hairpin net-shot very "tight", shuttle falls vertically close to opposite side of net, straight.

Half-smash hit at about half to three-quarter pace, often with an angled racket face (sliced).

Jump-smash body in the air to reach shuttle earlier by a one-footed leap to either side or two-footed straight up.

Lob high underarm clear from below net level.

Lunge final (or only) large "braking" step on to dominant leg when meeting shuttle wide of body.

Net-flick quick underarm clear met high at net flying flat to back court.

Net-interception "cut out" of drive, push or flick at net.

Net knock-off attacking net short, usually a "kill".

Pounce position-of-readiness straight-on defence in doubles mid-court or singles centre-court after hitting shuttle high – legs wide, knees flexed, on balls of feet, racket forward at about waist-height.

Punched-clear overhead forehand attacking clear hit hard and flatter to back court.

Push soft drive landing mid-court or close drop shot played from below tape height.

Round-the-head-shot hit from high backhand side with overhead forehand, footwork and hitting action.

Rushing-the-serve receiving a low serve with an attacking net shot often directly at opponents.

Scissor-kick overhead forehand footwork where legs change position in mid-air (lifting up off right foot, landing on left).

Side-on-defence turned partly sideways to defend mainly on one side of the body.

Spinner defensive net-shot where the "*outside*" of the shuttle base is stroked softly with an inward "caressing" movement causing it to *rotate* around its vertical axis.

Straight-on defence square to net to defend either side of the body.

Swipe (often called "Danish") backhand drive-clear played from mid- or back-court.

Tap forehand attacking net-shot, short action with no follow-through.

T meeting of front and middle lines.

Tumbler defensive net-shot where *underneath* of shuttle base is hit with a forward-jab movement causing it to *rotate* around its horizontal axis.

(See Diagram 1 for *court area* and *positional* terms)

Court Plan

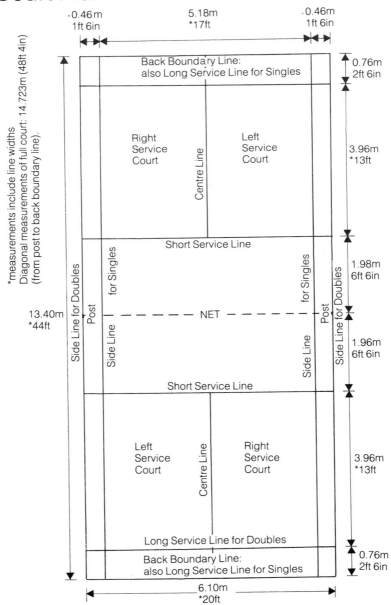

.0.46 m
1ft 6in

5.18m
*17ft

.0.46 m
1ft 6in

*measurements include line widths
Diagonal measurements of full court: 14.723m (48ft 4in)
(from post to back boundary line).

Back Boundary Line:
also Long Service Line for Singles

0.76m
2ft 6in

Right
Service
Court

Left
Service
Court

Centre Line

3.96m
*13ft

Short Service Line

Side Line for Doubles

for Singles

for Singles

Side Line for Doubles

1.98m
6ft 6in

Post

Side Line

NET

Side Line

Post

13.40m
*44ft

1.96m
6ft 6in

Short Service Line

Left
Service
Court

Centre Line

Right
Service
Court

3.96m
*13ft

Long Service Line for Doubles

Back Boundary Line:
also Long Service Line for Singles

0.76m
2ft 6in

6.10m
*20ft

Useful Addresses and Information

The governing bodies below organize competitions for all age groups and levels of play.

International Badminton Federation (IBF)
24 Winchcombe House
Winchcombe Street
Cheltenham, Glos.
Tel: 0242 34904
Formed in 1934. 83 affiliated countries to date. Monthly magazine issued.

Badminton Association of England (BA of E)
National Badminton Centre
Bradwell Road
Loughton Lodge
Milton Keynes MK8 9LA
Tel: 0908 568822
Formed in 1893 when game was formally instituted. Monthly magazine issued.
Coaches Register and bulletin.

English Schools Badminton Association (ESBA)
Operates from National Badminton Centre (address above). Formed in 1965 to encourage game in schools. Monthly information bulletin issued.

Badminton Union of Ireland (BU of I)
The House of Sport
Upper Malone Road
Belfast BT9 5LA
Tel: 0232 661222
Monthly magazine issued.
Coaches Register and bulletin.

Scottish Badminton Union (SBU)
Cockburn Centre
40 Bogmoor Place
Glasgow G51 4TQ
Tel: 041-445 1218
Monthly magazine issued.
Coaches Register and bulletin.

Welsh Badminton Union (WBU)
"Lynwood"
Tal-y-Garn
Pontyclun
Mid-Glamorgan CF7 9DA
Tel: 0443 22547

Badminton Instruction and Research Data Services (BIRDS)
c/o Wimbledon Badminton Centre
Cranbrook Road
London SW19 4BD
Tel: 01 947 5806
Professional coaching organization, run by author at UK's oldest private badminton club.

92

Index